D1220959

HorrorScapes

Witchcraft in Salem

by Steven L. Stern

Consultant: Alison D'Amario
Director of Education
Salem Witch Museum
Salem, Massachusetts

BEARPORT
PUBLISHING

New York, New York

Credits

Cover and title page illustration by Dawn Beard Creative and Kim Jones; 4–5, Kim Jones; 6, © The Granger Collection, New York; 7, © North Wind Picture Archives/Photolibrary; 8T, © North Wind Picture Archives/Alamy; 8B, © Massachusetts Historical Society, Boston, MA, USA/The Bridgeman Art Library International; 9, Kim Jones; 10, Kim Jones; 11L, Kim Jones; 11R, © North Wind Picture Archives/Alamy; 12, Kim Jones; 13, © Bettmann/Corbis; 14, Kim Jones; 15, Kim Jones; 16, © SuperStock; 17, © Briggs Co./George Eastman House/Getty Images; 18, © Peabody Essex Museum, Salem, Massachusetts, USA/The Bridgeman Art Library International; 19, © Peabody Essex Museum, Salem, Massachusetts, USA/The Bridgeman Art Library International; 20, © Peabody Essex Museum, Salem, Massachusetts, USA/The Bridgeman Art Library International; 21, Kim Jones; 22, © Collection of the New-York Historical Society, USA/The Bridgeman Art Library International; 23L, © The Granger Collection, New York; 23R, Courtesy of Department of History, Salem State College; 24, © Keitei/Wikimedia; 25L, © North Wind Picture Archives/Alamy; 25R, San Mateo Times, San Mateo, California, August 29, 1957 Copyright 2006 Heritage Microfilm, Inc. and Newspaperarchive.com; 27L, © Nigel Cattlin/Alamy; 27R, © Nina Leen//Time Life Pictures/Getty Images; 28L, © Erin Paul Donovan/Alamy; 28R, Courtesy of The Salem Massachusetts Police Department; 29L, © Richard B. Trask, Danvers, Massachusetts; 29R, © Richard B. Trask, Danvers, Massachusetts.

Publisher: Kenn Goin
Editorial Director: Adam Siegel
Creative Director: Spencer Brinker
Design: Dawn Beard Creative and Kim Jones
Illustrations: Kim Jones
Photo Researcher: Omni-Photo Communications, Inc.

Library of Congress Cataloging-in-Publication Data

Stern, Steven L.
  Witchcraft in Salem / by Steven L. Stern ; consultant, Alison D'Amario.
      p. cm. — (HorrorScapes)
  Includes bibliographical references and index.
  ISBN-13: 978-1-936088-00-3 (library binding)
  ISBN-10: 1-936088-00-2 (library binding)
  1. Trials (Witchcraft)—Massachusetts—Salem—History—17th century—Juvenile literature. 2. Witchcraft—Massachusetts—Salem—History—17th century—Juvenile literature. 3. Salem (Mass.)—History—Colonial period, ca. 1600–1775—Juvenile literature. I. Title.
  KFM2478.8.W5S84 2011
  133.4'3097445—dc22
                                    2010004683

For more information, write to Bearport Publishing Company, Inc., 101 Fifth Avenue, Suite 6R, New York, New York 10003. Printed in the United States of America in North Mankato, Minnesota.

062010
042110CGB

10 9 8 7 6 5 4 3 2 1

Contents

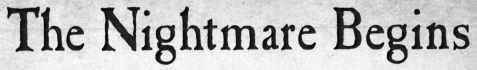

The Nightmare Begins

What was happening to Betty Parris and her cousin Abigail Williams? In January 1692, the two young girls began acting strangely. They crawled under chairs as if they were scared. They cried out and made odd sounds for no reason. Sometimes they flapped their arms like wings.

Betty's father, Reverend Samuel Parris, didn't know what to do. What awful illness could be causing this?

Abigail Williams lived with Betty Parris's family in Salem Village, Massachusetts. Only about 600 people lived in the small village.

Before long, things got worse. The girls started having **fits**. Their bodies would suddenly twist into crazy positions. They choked and screamed, as if under attack. Sometimes Betty would even bark like a dog!

Finally, in the middle of February, Reverend Parris asked Dr. William Griggs to examine the girls. Perhaps he could find the cause of their **bizarre** behavior. After observing them, Dr. Griggs said that the girls were "under an evil hand." Betty and Abigail were victims of **witchcraft**!

The doctor blamed the girls' strange behavior on witchcraft.

5

A Difficult Time

Unfortunately, the threat of witchcraft was not the only thing that made life difficult for the people of Salem Village in 1692. The winter that year was bitterly cold, and the dirt roads were often covered with snow. In addition, many people had recently died from **smallpox**. There was no cure for the deadly disease, and people feared that it might strike again.

Life was not easy in the 1600s. There was no electricity, running water, or cars. Families made almost everything they needed themselves, from houses and clothes to bread and butter.

Just as scary was the threat of an attack by **Native Americans**. The villagers lived on farms that were spread far apart. With no one close by to help, a deadly attack could come at any time.

The people of Salem were afraid that they might be attacked by Native Americans who lived in the nearby woods.

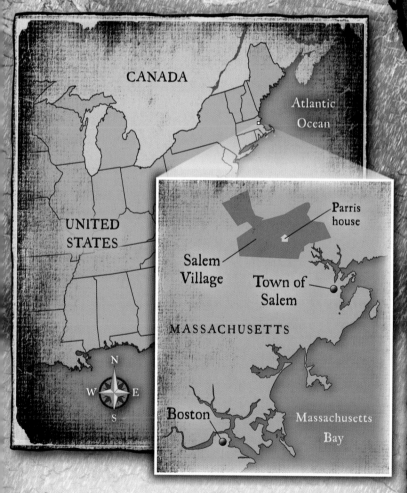

CANADA

Atlantic Ocean

UNITED STATES

Parris house

Salem Village

Town of Salem

MASSACHUSETTS

N
W E
S

Boston

Massachusetts Bay

Salem Village was about 5 miles (8 km) away from the town of Salem and 20 miles (32 km) north of Boston.

In 1692, Salem Village was part of the nearby town of Salem. Most of the people who lived in Salem Village were poor farmers. Many of the people in the town of Salem were rich **merchants** who traded **goods** with other merchants in England.

Forbidden Games

It wasn't easy for Betty and Abigail to find fun ways to spend the long, dark, candlelit days of winter. Reverend Parris did not allow the children to play games or have toys. He thought they were a waste of time and **sinful**. Games, he believed, were tools of the devil. Instead of playing, the girls should be cleaning and cooking, or reading the Bible. Betty and Abigail were bored, however. They secretly played fortune-telling games with their friends to pass the time.

Puritans on their way to church

Reverend Samuel Parris (left) and his family had moved to Salem Village in 1689 after he was hired to lead its church.

Like most people in Salem Village, Betty and Abigail were members of a religious group called Puritans. Puritans had strict rules and strong religious beliefs. For example, it was considered a sin not to attend church.

One day, the girls were playing a game with Abigail's friend, Ann Putnam. They dropped an egg white into a glass of water. Slowly, different shapes formed. The girls stared at them, watching for clues about the future and the men they might marry. Suddenly, a strange new shape appeared. The girls gasped. It looked like . . . a *coffin*!

They were horrified. What had they done? Surely this was an evil sign from the devil.

By playing the egg-and-glass game, Betty and Abigail knew they had broken the rules, risked punishment, and tempted the devil.

The Evil Spreads

It was in January 1692, shortly after Betty and Abigail saw the coffin during their fortune-telling game, when Reverend Parris began to notice that the girls were acting strangely. They stared into space and crawled on the ground for no reason. They complained of being pinched or stuck with invisible pins.

Even scarier, though, was that others also began acting **bewitched**. First was Ann Putnam. Before long, three more girls were affected. All had played forbidden games with Betty and Abigail—and now all were having fits.

The Puritans believed that witches were people who had made a bargain with the devil. In return for serving the devil, he granted them evil powers.

The devil was very real to the Puritans. They thought of him as a powerful, evil angel who fought against God.

Most people in Salem believed in witchcraft and the devil. They thought that with the devil's help, witches could cast **spells**, hurt people, and even kill them. As talk of the bewitched girls spread, the villagers became terrified. Evil **spirits** were at work, people whispered. Everyone was in great danger. Witchcraft was spreading through Salem!

In their sermons, Puritan ministers described how the devil and his servants were everywhere, ready to do evil.

During the 1600s, the preacher and writer Cotton Mather (above) warned of witchcraft and an "army of evil spirits" controlled by the devil. He believed that the bewitched girls were proof that the devil was at work in Salem.

Witches in Salem

Reverend Parris and others questioned the girls over and over. They demanded to know who was hurting them. At last, Betty named someone: Tituba.

Tituba was a South American Indian who had grown up on the island of Barbados (bar-BAY-dohs). She was now a slave in the Parris home.

Tituba helped care for Betty and Abigail.

Before long, other girls also named Tituba. *Who else?* the questioners asked again and again. *Who else?* The girls screamed and wept. They had more fits. Finally, they spoke two other names: Sarah Good and Sarah Osborne.

Village leaders took action. All three women were arrested and charged with witchcraft. There would be a **hearing**. If enough **evidence** was found, the women would go on **trial**. If they were found **guilty**, they would be hanged.

Sarah Good and Sarah Osborne were not well liked in Salem. Sarah Good was a homeless beggar with a bad temper. Sarah Osborne was a sick and weak older woman who had not gone to church in more than a year.

Sarah Osborne's house in Salem Village, which can still be seen there today

The Hearings Begin

At the beginning of March, the three **accused** women were brought to the meetinghouse in Salem Village. People crowded into the building to watch. Two judges asked the questions. The "bewitched" girls sat up front.

Sarah Good and Sarah Osborne denied they were witches. They said they had never hurt the children. Yet the girls insisted they had. Even worse, when the girls looked at the accused women, the girls screamed and fell to the floor, having fits. The judges were convinced. They ordered both women to be sent to jail.

Accused witches were chained to the walls of dirty, dark prison cells. Sometimes they were tortured.

Tituba was next. People had questioned her many times, and now the judges were shouting at her again. The girls continued to have fits. Tituba was scared. Finally, she told the judges what they wanted to hear. She **confessed** to being a witch. The judges then sent her to prison as well.

People accused of being witches were not hanged if they admitted their crime. Because Tituba confessed to being a witch, she was not in danger of being killed.

During Tituba's confession, she talked about seeing a red rat, a black rat, and a mysterious tall man with white hair who dressed in black.

A Death Sentence

Three accused witches were now in jail. Yet that was just the beginning. Abigail Williams, Ann Putnam, and the other girls kept having fits and naming more people. The accused often named other people, claiming they were witches. Some of the accused were even respected members of the community. That didn't protect them, however. Soon the jails overflowed with accused witches awaiting trial.

A father tries to protect his daughter who is accused of being a witch.

The proof of witchcraft was often little more than **spectral evidence**. This evidence meant that accusers claimed that the specter, or spirit, of a supposed witch attacked them, even though that person wasn't close by.

In June 1692, the Salem witch trials began. The first person tried was Bridget Bishop. She hoped her trial would end better than her hearing. Unfortunately, it didn't. People **testified** against her. The girls screamed, cried, and fell to the ground.

The jury considered the evidence and found Bridget guilty. The judges sentenced her to death. Eight days later, Bridget Bishop was hanged.

Bridget Bishop was the first person to be hanged.

Witches on Trial

In late June, five more women went on trial. One was 71-year-old Rebecca Nurse. Many people were shocked when she was accused. Rebecca was a kind, gentle, religious woman.

At her trial, relatives, friends, and neighbors spoke in Rebecca's defense. To their relief, the jury found her not guilty. However, when the **verdict** was read, the bewitched girls went into violent fits! Many people in the courtroom also cried out.

Accused witches were often searched for a "witch's mark," or "devil's mark," on their bodies. The marks found were usually what would now be called birthmarks, warts, or moles.

This painting shows people searching for a witch's mark on an accused witch's back.

The judges told the jury to think things over again. They did—and this time they found Rebecca guilty.

The other four women were also found guilty. All were sentenced to die.

More trials followed. Again and again the accused were found guilty. Even a four-year-old girl, Sarah Good's daughter, was sent to jail!

During a trial, the bewitched girls often had fits, as shown in this painting. The fits were frightening to see. The girls seemed to be truly suffering.

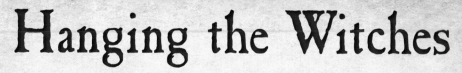

Hanging the Witches

In the three months after Bridget Bishop was **executed**, 18 more women and men were hanged. Many people came to watch the hangings. A wooden cart carried the prisoners, in chains, up the steep, rocky slope of Gallows Hill. People shouted at the prisoners and called them names.

This painting shows accused witches being brought to Gallows Hill.

At the top of the hill the prisoners waited to be hung either from a **gallows** or a large tree. One by one, the executioner tightened a **noose** around their necks and then hung them. The families of the victims then took the bodies home so that they could be privately buried.

At his trial, 80-year-old Giles Corey refused to cooperate with the court. To force him to speak, guards put him face-up on the ground and began piling heavy rocks on his chest. Giles stubbornly kept silent as he was crushed to death.

Giles Corey being crushed under stones

The Witch Hunt Ends

By fall of 1692, doubts about the trials and hangings were growing. More and more voices spoke out against the witch hunt. People especially questioned spectral evidence. They said it couldn't be trusted. After all, couldn't the devil create the specter of an *innocent* person? One leading minister said, "It were better that ten suspected witches should escape, than that one innocent person should be condemned." Others agreed.

An accused witch being brought to Gallows Hill

Finally, on October 29, 1692, Governor William Phips of Massachusetts took action. He shut down the court. A new one was formed in its place, but this court would require true proof of guilt. Spectral evidence would no longer be allowed. Without it, most accused people were found not guilty. In May 1693, Phips **pardoned** the prisoners still in jail.

William Phips was the governor of Massachusetts in 1692.

An accused witch in prison

At the time the governor acted, about 200 people had been accused of being a witch—including the governor's own wife!

After the Trials

The Salem witch trials lasted less than a year. Yet during that time, 20 people were killed for witchcraft. At least 5 others died in prison. Many people's lives were ruined.

Even after being pardoned, some prisoners were stuck in jail. The law said they could not get out until they paid their jail costs. Some had to sell their farms to raise the money.

In Memory of
Wilmot Redd
of Marblehead
An innocent victim of the
Salem Witchcraft Trials
Hung on September 22
1692

Wilmot Redd was one of eight people hanged on September 22, 1692. These hangings were the last ones.

Years later, in 1697, one of the Salem judges, Samuel Sewall, wrote a letter in which he apologized for his part in the witch trials. Some **jurors** also said they were sorry. As for the bewitched girls, only one asked for forgiveness. In 1706, Ann Putnam explained that the devil had tricked her. She said she was sorry for having accused "innocent persons."

Judge Samuel Sewall's letter asking for forgiveness for his "blame and shame" is read aloud.

Legislature Erases Witch-Convictions

BOSTON (AP) — The state of Massachusetts has wiped from the books the conviction of six women unjustly accused of being witches 265 years ago.

Gov. Foster Furcolo signed a legislative resolve clearing Ann Pudeator, Bri⸻ Bishop, Alice Parker Sus⸻ ⸻rtin, Mar-

In 1957, the state of Massachusetts formally apologized for what happened in 1692 and cleared the names of some of the accused witches. In 2001, more than 300 years after the witch trials began, the rest of the accused were officially cleared.

Why Did It Happen?

What had caused the Salem witch hunt? **Historians** have various ideas. Many think that Thomas Putnam, Ann Putnam's father, used charges of witchcraft to attack people he didn't like. Thomas Putnam signed almost half of the legal complaints against accused witches. His daughter Ann charged more than 60 people with witchcraft.

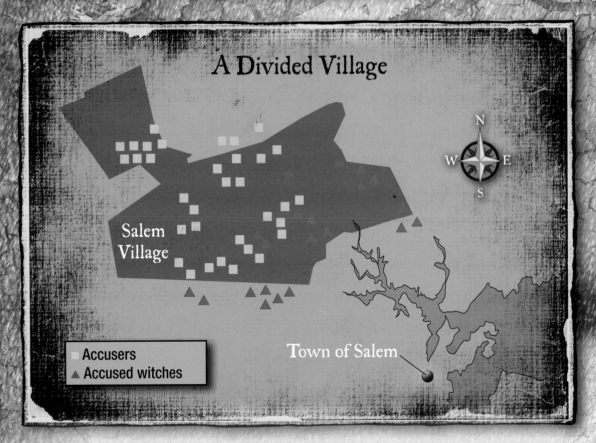

A Divided Village

N
W · E
S

Salem
Village

Town of Salem

■ Accusers
▲ Accused witches

Many farmers in the western part of Salem Village didn't want to remain part of the town of Salem. They felt that the merchants there did not live according to Puritan values. Many people in the eastern part of Salem Village, however, were merchants. They wanted to remain part of the town. Could that be one of the reasons so many of them were accused of being witches by their western neighbors?

Another theory is that the bewitched girls suffered from **hysteria**. This illness is brought on by extreme fear. Hysteria can have mental and physical symptoms. As a result, the girls' fear of the devil and witches could have caused them to have fits. Hysteria can also spread to other people during stressful times. This might explain why many Salem villagers were affected.

The exact cause may never be known. Yet one thing is certain. After the Salem witch hunt ended, no one in the United States was ever killed for being a witch again.

ergot

Some people believe that the bewitched girls ate rye bread infected by the **fungus** ergot. This fungus can cause **hallucinations**. As a result, the girls may have seen and heard things that weren't real.

This monument was built in 1885 to honor Rebecca Nurse, who was hanged during the Salem witch trials.

SALEM:
Then and Now

Then: Salem was made up of Salem Village and the town of Salem.

Now: Salem Village is called Danvers. It changed its name in 1752 so that it would no longer be reminded of its dark history. The town of Salem is now called the city of Salem.

Then: During the time of the witch trials, about 600 people lived in Salem Village.

Now: About 25,000 people live in Danvers today.

The city of Salem's police department uses the image of a witch on a broomstick.

Then: "Spectral evidence" was allowed to accuse people of being witches.

Now: Imaginary evidence cannot be used to send people to jail. The law in the United States protects an accused person's right to a fair trial.

SALEM WITCH MUSEUM

Today, people come to the Salem Witch Museum to learn about the shocking events that took place in Salem more than 300 years ago.

Then: Witchcraft was considered a crime.

Now: Witchcraft is no longer considered a crime. In fact, a form of witchcraft called Wicca (WIK-uh) is practiced as a religion.

Then: The town of Salem was the site of the trials and hangings of accused witches.

Now: The city of Salem welcomes tourists to what it calls "The Witch City." Visitors come to see such places as Gallows Hill and the Salem Witch Museum.

Then: The Salem Village meetinghouse was used as a place to examine accused witches, including Sarah Good, Sarah Osborne, and Tituba.

Now: Across the street from where the meetinghouse once stood is a memorial honoring the victims of the witch trials. It was built in 1992.

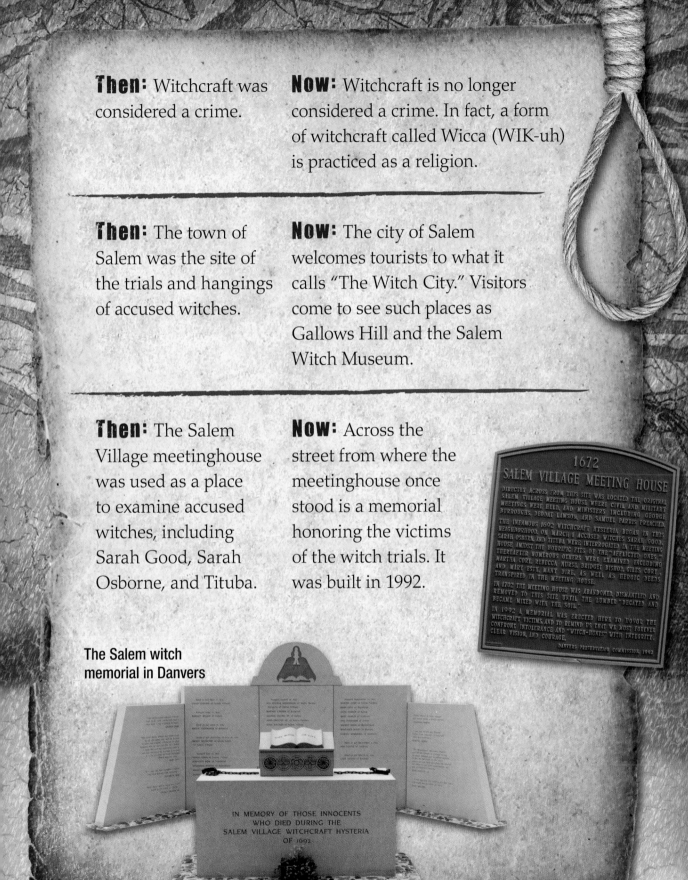

1672
SALEM VILLAGE MEETING HOUSE

DIRECTLY ACROSS FROM THIS SITE WAS LOCATED THE ORIGINAL SALEM VILLAGE MEETING HOUSE WHERE CIVIL AND MILITARY MEETINGS WERE HELD, AND MINISTERS INCLUDING GEORGE BURROUGHS, DEODAT LAWSON, AND SAMUEL PARRIS PREACHED.

THE INFAMOUS 1692 WITCHCRAFT HYSTERIA BEGAN IN THIS NEIGHBORHOOD. ON MARCH 1 ACCUSED WITCHES SARAH GOOD, SARAH OSBORN, AND TITUBA WERE INTERROGATED IN THE MEETING HOUSE AMIDST THE HORRIFIC FITS OF THE "AFFLICTED ONES." THEREAFTER NUMEROUS OTHERS WERE EXAMINED INCLUDING MARTHA COREY, REBECCA NURSE, BRIDGET BISHOP, GILES COREY, AND MARY ESTY. MANY DIRE, AS WELL AS HEROIC DEEDS TRANSPIRED IN THE MEETING HOUSE.

IN 1702 THE MEETING HOUSE WAS ABANDONED, DISMANTLED AND REMOVED TO THIS SITE UNTIL THE LUMBER "DECAYED AND BECAME MIXED WITH THE SOIL."

IN 1992 A MEMORIAL WAS ERECTED HERE TO HONOR THE WITCHCRAFT VICTIMS, AND TO REMIND US THAT WE MUST FOREVER CONFRONT INTOLERANCE AND "WITCH-HUNTS" WITH INTEGRITY, CLEAR VISION, AND COURAGE.

DANVERS PRESERVATION COMMISSION, 1992

The Salem witch memorial in Danvers

IN MEMORY OF THOSE INNOCENTS
WHO DIED DURING THE
SALEM VILLAGE WITCHCRAFT HYSTERIA
OF 1692

29

Glossary

accused (uh-KYOOZD) blamed for or charged with a crime or for doing something wrong

bewitched (bi-WICHT) affected by witchcraft; placed under a spell

bizarre (bi-ZAR) very strange or odd

coffin (KAWF-in) a long box in which a dead person is buried

confessed (kuhn-FEST) admitted that one has done something wrong

evidence (EV-uh-duhnss) information and facts that can be used to prove whether something is true

executed (EK-suh-*kyoo*-tid) put to death

fits (FITS) sudden outbursts or attacks of something that cannot be controlled

fungus (FUHN-guhss) a plant-like organism, such as a mushroom, that cannot make its own food

gallows (GAL-ohz) a wooden structure used to hang criminals

goods (GUDZ) things that are sold

guilty (GIL-tee) having done something wrong or against the law

hallucinations (huh-*loo*-suh-NAY-shuhnz) seeing or hearing things that aren't there

hearing (HEER-ing) a presentation before a judge to review information and decide whether there should be a trial

historians (his-TOR-ee-uhnz) people who study past events

hysteria (hi-STEHR-ee-uh) a condition in which fear or panic keeps a person from thinking clearly

jurors (JUR-urz) people who serve on a jury

merchants (MUR-chuhnts) people who sell goods

Native Americans (NAY-tiv uh-MER-uh-kinz) the first people to live in America; they are sometimes called American Indians

noose (NOOSS) a large loop at the end of a piece of rope

pardoned (PAR-duhnd) excused or forgave; released a person from punishment

sinful (SIN-ful) behavior that is wrong according to one's religious laws or beliefs

smallpox (SMAWL-poks) an often deadly disease that spreads from one person to another; it causes fevers and painful pimple-like sores that often leave scars

spectral evidence (SPEK-truhl EV-uh-duhnss) proof of witchcraft based on a person's claim of having seen a witch's spirit

spells (SPELZ) words that are supposed to have magical powers

spirits (SPIHR-its) supernatural creatures, such as ghosts

testified (TES-tuh-fyed) gave evidence in a court of law

trial (TRYE-uhl) an examination of evidence in a court of law to decide if a charge is true

verdict (VUR-dikt) a decision given to the court by a jury

witchcraft (WICH-kraft) the actions or magical powers of a witch

Bibliography

Hill, Frances. *A Delusion of Satan: The Full Story of the Salem Witch Trials.* New York: Da Capo Press (2002).

Roach, Marilynne K. *The Salem Witch Trials: A Day-by-Day Chronicle of a Community Under Seige.* New York: Cooper Square Press (2002).

Rosenthal, Bernard. *Salem Story: Reading the Witch Trials of 1692.* New York: Cambridge University Press (1998).

www.salemwitchmuseum.com/

www.salemwitchtrials.org/home.html

Read More

Fradin, Judith Bloom and Dennis Brindell. *The Salem Witch Trials.* Tarrytown, NY: Marshall Cavendish (2009).

Kent, Deborah. *Witchcraft Trials: Fear, Betrayal, and Death in Salem.* Berkeley Heights, NJ: Enslow Publishers (2009).

Magoon, Kekla. *The Salem Witch Trials.* Edina, MN: ABDO Publishing Company (2008).

Nardo, Don. *The Salem Witch Trials.* Detroit, MI: Lucent Books (2007).

Price, Sean. *Salem Witch Trials.* Chicago: Raintree (2009).

von Zumbusch, Amelie. *The True Story of the Salem Witch Hunts.* New York: PowerKids Press (2009).

Yolen, Jane, and Elisabeth Yolen Stemple. *The Salem Witch Trials: An Unsolved Mystery from History.* New York: Simon & Schuster Books for Young Readers (2004).

Learn More Online

To learn more about the Salem witch trials, visit
www.bearportpublishing.com/HorrorScapes

Index

About the Author

Steven L. Stern has more than 30 years of experience as a writer and editor developing textbooks, learning materials, and works of nonfiction and fiction for children and adults. He is the author of 22 books as well as numerous articles and short stories. He has also worked as a teacher, a lexicographer, and a writing consultant.